WILD ANIMALS
IN CAPTIVITY
ROB LAIDLAW

Kudu, Heidelberg, Germany. Volker Seding/Courtesy of Stephen Bulger Gallery

Fitzhenry & Whiteside

Praise for *Wild Animals in Captivity*

"After two centuries of public acceptance, the tide is finally turning against zoos. In this honest, plain-speaking critique, zoo expert Rob Laidlaw explains why, in the words of Axel Munthe, 'The wild, cruel beast is not behind the bars of the cage. He is in front of it.'"
—*Jonathan Balcombe, Ph.D., Author,* Pleasurable Kingdom: Animals and the Nature of Feeling Good

"Rob Laidlaw writes about what every young person, with their natural empathy, instinctively feels—that animals suffer horribly in zoos and, even with our best efforts, we cannot alleviate that misery or justify their incarceration. Dramatically and powerfully presented with stark comparisons between animals' natural lives and often-heartbreaking cases of individual animals in zoos (few people will be able to quickly forget Yupi the polar bear), this book will set kids on the path to compassion and advocacy."
—*Ingrid Newkirk, President, People for the Ethical Treatment of Animals*

"A very important book. Rob Laidlaw presents a balanced view of life in captivity for sentient beings who would rather be free. Just like humans, animals have a point of view and preferences for what happens to them. Much of the time what humans call 'good welfare' isn't good enough—we can always do better for zoo residents and other animals. One way to make the world a more compassionate and less cruel place is to teach children well. And this is exactly what this book does. Children are ambassadors for the future, and keeping their hopes and dreams for a better world alive will translate into increasing our compassion footprint. I will share this book widely in my work with Roots & Shoots (http://www.rootsandshoots.org) groups around the world."
—*Marc Bekoff, Professor Emeritus of Ecology and Evolutionary Biology, the University of Colorado; co-founder with Jane Goodall of Ethnologists for the Ethical Treatment of Animals, authors of* The Ten Trusts; *Author,* The Emotional Lives of Animals; Animals Matter; *and* Animals at Play: Rules of the Game

"This little book is deceptively powerful. It asks young people to look objectively at what they see in zoos, and to think about what zoo animals need and want. Laidlaw cuts through the marketing doublespeak of many modern zoos, and in plain language he asks questions that need to be considered not only by a new generation, but also by zoos themselves."
—*David Hancocks, Author,* A Different Nature: The Paradoxical World of Zoos and Their Uncertain Future. *Former Director, Woodland Park Zoo (Seattle, Washington); Arizona-Sonora Desert Museum (Tucson, Arizona); Werribee Open Range Zoo (Melbourne, Australia)*

"It is time for a new generation to take a critical look at zoos. Had the young people of Anchorage heard Laidlaw's ideas, they might have asked key questions about the role of their own zoo, and Maggie the elephant's suffering could have ended much sooner. An irresistible read for all ages!"
—*Friends of Maggie, Anchorage, Alaska*

"This is the best book I have ever read about zoos for children. I can think of nothing more educational than giving this book to every child before visiting a zoo… A must for every parent or teacher who wants their children to learn the truth about zoos."
—*Jeffrey Moussaieff Masson, Author,* When Elephants Weep: The Emotional Lives of Animals; Dogs Never Lie About Love: Reflections on the Emotional World of Dogs; *and* The Pig Who Sang to the Moon: The Emotional Lives of Farm Animals

"If there ever was a book that taught empathy, compassion, and respect for our fellow beings, that captured the spirit and essence of the varied species with whom we share our planet, this [book] is certainly it. Through personal stories and observations, Rob Laidlaw has beautifully juxtaposed the quality of the lives of animals in the wild to those in captivity. This splendid book will open up the hearts, minds, and awareness of its readers, young and old, to the beauty of animals, and to the terrible plight of so many of them in captivity. Beautifully, we are educated as to the ways their lives can and should be improved. It is clearly one of the best books on animals, be they in the wild or in captivity, that I have ever read. Its clear information and powerful message must spread to young and old alike."
—*Elliot M. Katz, DVM President, In Defense of Animals*

"For the first time this is a book that encourages children to question—rather than accept—what they see and to look at captivity through the eyes of those on the other side of the bars. It nurtures the spark of conscience that something is wrong in so many zoos today and offers both insight and opportunity for putting it right. This book will compel zoo directors and visitors alike to question the value of captivity—not from any conservation perspective—but purely and simply from the physical and emotional needs of the animals themselves. When we can look these animals in the eyes and know they are content we will have done our job."
—*Jill Robinson MBE, Founder & CEO, Animals Asia Foundation*

"A brilliant introduction to the welfare of animals in zoos. [This] book is well researched, thought-provoking, and an essential read for all young people. It will make you think twice the next time you see an animal in the zoo and wonder if we should indeed keep wildlife in the wild. This book is an essential handbook for all budding zoo-checkers or anyone interested in making a positive difference in the lives of captive animals."
—*Louis Ng, Executive Director, Animal Concerns Research and Education Society (ACRES), Singapore*

CONTENTS

Leopard, Usti, Czech Republic. Volker Seding / Stephen Bulger Gallery

INTRODUCTION

The first zoo I visited as a kid was the Riverdale Zoo in Toronto. It was an old zoo located close to the heart of the city on a hillside with lots of big trees. Not much had changed since it opened in 1894.

Monkeys and apes were displayed behind bars in small cages in the ancient-looking primate building. Wild cats and bears occupied concrete cages in the carnivore house. Zebras, camels, and deer lived in dusty, fenced outdoor pens, and birds were confined in cages where they had no room to fly.

I especially remember one big silverback gorilla who sat alone in a dark, concrete room behind steel bars and thick glass. There was nothing for him to climb or play with. I spent a lot of time looking into his eyes, trying to make a connection because he looked so sad. I wondered if he had been captured in the wild and torn away from his family, and how long he had been living behind bars.

Like most kids, I was fascinated by wild animals. I read a lot about how they lived in their natural habitats—how they spent their days finding food, communicating, caring for their families, and playing with each other. Unlike the wild animals in my books, the animals in the zoo didn't really do anything. Mostly they sat staring out of their cages.

I went back to the Riverdale Zoo seven or eight times with my family and classmates, but I didn't like it very much. I always left the zoo feeling sorry for the animals.

Today, as the director of Zoocheck Canada, I visit all sorts of zoos. Zoocheck Canada was established in 1984 to protect the welfare of wild animals living in captivity. Part of my job is to convince governments to pass better laws to regulate zoos and improve the lives of captive wild animals. Another part involves challenging outdated and cruel zoo practices and the keeping of wildlife in captivity. My visits have taken me to the worst zoos—roadside zoos where wild animals live in small, barren cages. And to the best zoos—like the Arizona-Sonora Desert Museum and the Jersey Zoo—where wild animals live in diverse and stimulating habitats.

City of Toronto Archives

The Riverdale Zoo in Toronto in the 1920s

4

More than 20 years of zoo investigations, studies, and campaigns have convinced me that it's best to keep wildlife in the wild and that most zoos should close. At the same time, we have a responsibility to do whatever we can to give those animals now held captive in zoos a better life.

This book describes some of the problems of keeping wild animals in captivity and some ideas for fixing them. Learning more about the lives of captive wild animals will help you look at zoos and the animals they keep in a different way. Maybe the next time you visit a zoo, you'll start asking questions. Do the giraffes have enough space to roam around? Are the polar bears suffering because it's hot and humid? Why are the lions pacing back and forth?

Asking those kinds of questions is the first step in getting involved, doing something to improve the lives of wild animals in captivity. And that's what feeds my hope for the future—people working together to ensure that all wild animals are treated with respect and compassion.

CHAPTER 1

Living in Captivity

Two Brown Lizards

A few years ago, I traveled to the city of Kuala Lumpur in Malaysia to visit Zoo Negara. It's a large zoo spread over 45 hectares (110 acres). The zoo's exhibits included 400 species of mammals, birds, reptiles, amphibians, and fish—a total of more than 5000 animals. But it was two small brown lizards that grabbed my attention that day.

I was sitting on a stone bench in one of the zoo's shady gardens when I saw the first lizard. He was perched on a low rock wall just a few steps away. I had no idea what kind of lizard he was. For nearly 15 minutes, he moved all around the garden. He stopped, looked here and there, and then scurried off in sudden bursts of energy. He traveled in one direction and then another, climbing walls and trees, running, jumping, and catching insects.

Later that day, I encountered the second lizard. He looked the same as the first lizard—about 20 centimeters (8 inches) long with faint stripes down his back. He was in an exhibit that looked like a small aquarium. It was about twice as long as he was and contained a couple of branches and a rock. I watched that lizard for 15 minutes. He didn't run, climb, jump, or do much of anything.

How different the lives of those two brown lizards were. The first lizard lived in a natural habitat and was always busy exploring his environment, deciding where to go, what to eat, when to rest. The second lizard lived in captivity. He spent his days alone and inactive in a zoo exhibit, being gawked at by noisy crowds of people. That's not much of a life for a lizard.

Even small animals, like this changeable lizard, need space and stimulation for natural movements and behaviors.

Nick Barker/www.ecologyasia.com

Captive Lives

What does living in captivity mean? For fish, lizards, birds, dolphins, gorillas, and other wild animals living in zoos, it means a life that is completely dependent on people. Zoo owners, zoo directors, and zookeepers decide what kind of exhibit the animals live in; how deep they can swim, how high they can fly, or how far they can walk; what and when they eat; which companions or mates they have.

Decisions are often based on how much space zoos have and which species attract the most visitors—not on the animals' needs. When that happens, wild animals suffer from living in captivity. For a better life, they require the kinds of natural and complex experiences all animals encounter in the wild.

Most zoos own the animals they buy or breed. And most laws consider animals their owner's property, like a toaster or a tennis racket.

Acting Naturally

Dereck Bryceson

We've learned a lot about the lives of wild animals from field scientists who have studied them in their natural habitats. They include people like chimpanzee expert Jane Goodall, PhD, DBE (above); elephant experts Winnie Kiiru (above), Iain Douglas-Hamilton, and Cynthia Moss; and Lynn Rogers, the world's leading authority on black bears.

From the work of field scientists, we know that wild animals have very complex lives. They spend most of their time doing whatever they need to do in order to survive—hunting for food and water, finding mates, raising families, evading predators, exploring and patrolling their territory. But their lives are much richer than that. Many species develop deep social and family bonds that last a lifetime, and some—such as apes, whales, and elephants—communicate and express many of the same emotions as we do.

At home in the wild, animals have control over their lives. They're acting naturally—roaming around their territory, using their skills and knowledge, caring for their families. In captivity, animals have no control, and most live in exhibits that are nothing like home. Just ask a polar bear who's living on a concrete floor in tropical temperatures, rather than on ice floes in the Arctic. Or an elephant who's living with one companion, rather than a dozen grandmothers, aunts, and siblings. It's hard to act naturally in zoo exhibits that have no sea ice or elephant aunts.

When they can't act naturally, wild animals may end up sick and unfit. They may also develop abnormal behaviors because they feel bored and frustrated.

Unnatural Behavior

At many of the zoos I visit, I see animals doing things their species never do in the wild. I've noticed tigers and other animals lying down and sleeping their days away. I've found monkeys frantically pulling out their hair and playing with their feces.

I've also watched elephants rocking back and forth, bears pacing in a figure-eight pattern, monkeys climbing in a continuous loop, and dolphins swimming in endless circles. These repetitive behaviors are called stereotypies, and they are often a sign that the animals feel frustrated and have nothing else to do.

When wild animals are inactive or behaving unnaturally, their space at the zoo is probably much too small and not stimulating enough.

Holly Penfound

Zoos say their animal displays are educational, but there's not much evidence to support that claim. Not a lot can be learned by looking at caged animals, especially when they are acting abnormally, like this pacing coyote.

Room to Roam

Wild animals in captivity need a lot of room to walk, run, climb, fly, or swim the same way their species do in the wild. But most live in very small spaces.

In the wild, many animals are on the move all day, and it isn't just because they're hungry, thirsty, or need a place to rest. Winnie Kiiru has observed a family of elephants walking more than 16 kilometers (10 miles) each night to a favorite resting place, even though a suitable one was nearby. Carol Buckley, co-founder of the Elephant Sanctuary in Tennessee, says the retired elephants she looks after often travel out of their way to splash around in a favorite swimming hole or to a special patch of forest for no obvious reason.

All this movement tones muscles and strengthens bones, and wild animals need to be fit and healthy to survive. But wild animals also travel for many reasons that we don't really understand—reasons that are important to the animals and necessary for their well-being.

Nearly every zoo keeps animals in exhibits that are far smaller than the animals need. Jordi Casamitjana investigated the living spaces of elephants in British zoos, and found them more

When elephants stand around all day on hard surfaces, they often develop arthritis and foot infections. Zoo elephants die because of foot infections every year.

Rob Laidlaw

than 1000 times smaller than their natural home range. Wild polar bears sometimes travel 50-100 kilometers (31-67 miles) in a day hunting for seals, but zoos confine them in spaces that are more than a million times smaller than their Arctic territory.

At a zoo in India, this lion lives in a large natural exhibit with room to roam and places to hide.

Places to Hide

In the wild, animals need places to hide. They hide to avoid predators, when they give birth and raise their families, and when it's time for a rest. Animals in captivity have even more reasons to hide. They need a break from all the foreign noises, sights, and smells of a zoo full of visitors. When they can't escape to a private spot, animals suffer from anxiety and stress. That can lead to aggression against other animals and zookeepers. Stressed animals also find ways to hurt themselves. Some monkeys, for example, chew their fingers or tails to the bone.

Something to Do

In 2005, I watched two wild black bears in Banff National Park in Alberta. For more than 30 minutes they meandered along a shallow riverbed. They turned over stones, pulled apart logs, chased each other through the water, then climbed a distant ridge and disappeared over the top.

The bears were energetic and full of life. As they explored the area, they seemed interested in everything. They observed, smelled, listened, and touched. They interacted with each other and their environment, and were always busy making choices about what to do and where to go.

What's there for captive bears to do in a zoo? In many zoos, bears live in small, barren exhibits. Because there's nothing to challenge and stimulate them, many end up pacing back and forth or sleeping all day.

Life is empty and barren for the bears living in this concrete enclosure.

Rob Laidlaw

Other zoos have been trying to make life more interesting for their animals by filling their exhibits with structures, equipment, and other objects. Behind this is the idea, called environmental enrichment, that captive animals will move naturally and act normally if zoos provide them with things to explore and

This exhibit is filled with natural structures and furniture to make the bears' lives more interesting.

13

challenges to sort out. Ensuring that social animals have opportunities to bond and interact is another important part of environmental enrichment.

Since the 1980s, zoos have installed high platforms for lions to perch on; wooden structures for bears to climb; trees and rope ladders for monkeys to swing from; large hanging objects for rhinos to push against; and mud baths for hippos to wallow in. Some zoo exhibits also include other furniture and toys.

Giving animals something to do is important, but environmental enrichment can't fix everything. It doesn't really help captive animals living in a space that's too small for natural behavior. For other animals, interest in the same old toys and furniture doesn't last long. Things must be changed frequently to give the animals fresh objects to explore.

It's important to remember that the best environments don't need enrichment at all because they are already large, interesting, and complex enough. If a a cage needs a lot of enrichment, it's probably too small and too artificial for the animals.

Animal Furniture

Zookeepers need to be creative in finding large equipment and objects, called furniture, that stimulate each species' natural behavior. This is some of the common furniture I've seen in zoo exhibits around the world: fir-tree mountains, log piles, rock piles, leaf piles, sandboxes, tubes, perches, hammocks, wooden rings, scratching posts, sprinklers, kegs, boomer balls, traffic cones, cardboard boxes, tires, ice blocks, animal carcasses and skins, animal scents, animal sounds, scattered seeds, Popsicles and other food treats.

A Good Life?

Rob Laidlaw

Can wild animals have a good life in captivity? It can never be as interesting or complex as the wild, but some species can be kept healthy, active, and alert.

To do that, zoos must make the welfare of the animals their top priority. Supplying nutritious food, fresh water, and veterinary care is the easy part. Much tougher is creating an environment that gives captive animals lots of opportunities to act like wild animals.

How can you tell if a zoo animal's quality of life is good or bad? Answering that question can start with the Five Freedoms of Animal Welfare. The Five Freedoms originated in the 1960s in Britain to protect farm animals. Since then, they have been used by governments and animal organizations around the world to assess wild animal welfare.

Five Freedoms

For a sense of well-being, animals living in captivity need these
five freedoms:

1. Freedom from thirst, hunger, and malnutrition
   (nutritious food and fresh water)

2. Freedom from discomfort
   (appropriate shelter and comfortable climate)

3. Freedom from pain, injury, and disease
   (gentle treatment and veterinary care)

4. Freedom to express normal behavior
   (large natural space and rich environment)

5. Freedom from fear and distress
   (places to hide and respectful zookeepers)

This javelina is enjoying the
Five Freedoms in a natural
desert habitat at the Arizona-
Sonora Desert Museum.

15

Rob Laidlaw

CHAPTER 2

Challenging Animals

Polar bears, elephants, dolphins (including orcas), and the Great Apes do not belong in zoos. They have special and challenging needs, including vast, natural spaces, and most need the company of large families.

Polar Bears

Lynn and Donna Rogers

Natural Facts

Home: Home is the pack ice that rims the Arctic Ocean, where winter temperatures drop to –40 degrees C (–40 degrees F) and summer temperatures peak at 10 degrees C (50 degrees F). Bears can inhabit a home range that's twice the size of Iceland.

Size: Adult males weigh 300-600 kilograms (660-1300 pounds) and stand 3 meters (11 feet) high. Adult females are half the size of males. Newborn cubs weigh about 600 grams (1 pound).

Adaptations: Polar bears are equipped for comfort in the cold. Under their black skin, which absorbs heat from the sun, is a thick layer of fat. An inner coat of soft fur and an outer coat of hollow guard hairs insulate their skin. Polar bears start overheating when temperatures rise above 10 degrees C (50 degrees F).

Family Life: One or two cubs are born in November and December. Cubs stay with their mothers for two years. Adult bears hunt and live on their own.

Conservation status: Threatened species, due to global warming, pollution, hunting, and other threats.

In the Wild

The seal rested close to her breathing hole, a small circle of open water in a sea of thick arctic ice. She kept a watchful eye on the landscape of snow drifts and ice jumbles. Suddenly, in a silent explosion of energy, a polar bear pounced at the seal from behind a snow rise. She slipped into her hole and dove down.

The bear had just spent the last hour slowly pushing the snow rise ahead of him. Now he sat patiently at the breathing hole, knowing the seal would have to surface for air. Fifteen minutes later, the bear caught his meal. After devouring 30 kilograms (66 pounds) of seal meat, he set off for a distant ice ridge. He moved from one floating ice pan to another. Sometimes he slipped into the water and paddled forward with his huge paws.

When he reached the ice ridge, the bear scrambled to the top, scraped a depression in the snow, and climbed in to sleep. Far out on the pack ice was a female polar bear with her two cubs. She had given birth at the edge of the boreal forest more than 100 kilometers (62 miles) to the south. For three months, she had been feeding on seals, birds' eggs, and berries. Once the summer heat melts the ice, she'll have to wait for new ice to form in the fall to hunt for seals again.

In Captivity

It was early morning, but the polar bear was already hot from the tropical sun. He'd been captured as an orphan in the Arctic three years before and shipped to a tropical zoo that wanted a polar bear cub.

To escape the sun, the bear moved to a shady spot and laid on the concrete floor with his legs splayed out. The hot, humid weather had taken its toll. There were patches of green in the bear's white fur, where algae were growing inside his hollow guard hairs.

When his shade disappeared, the bear began pacing back and forth. He walked in one direction, thrust his head straight up, twisted it around, and paced back in the other direction. Each foot fell in the same place every time.

These polar bears live in a tropical zoo in Indonesia. The hot, humid climate has produced patches of green algae in their hollow guard hairs.

Rob Laidlaw

Natural Facts

Home: Asian elephants live in the tropical forests of India, Sri Lanka, Indonesia, and Southeast Asia. African elephants are at home on the savannas and in the forests of central and southern Africa. Families of Kenyan elephants roam territories that range from 100 to 5000 square kilometers (about 40 to 1900 square miles).

Size: Male Asian elephants weigh up to 5000 kilograms (about 11,000 pounds) and stand 3 meters (10 feet) high at the shoulder. Male African elephants weigh 6000 kilograms (13,000 pounds) and stand 4 meters (13 feet) high. In both species, females are about half the size of males.

Adaptations: Elephants are equipped for comfort in hot climates and vast territories. Blood vessels in their huge ears act like a cooling system. Their column-like legs and padded feet are designed for carrying heavy weight over great distances. Intelligence, long memories, affection, and the ability to communicate hold elephant families together.

Family Life: Female members of a family of 10-15 elephants live together for lifetimes and generations and form deep emotional bonds. When they're about 13 years old, young males join bachelor groups. Sometimes several families move together as clans.

Conservation status: Endangered or vulnerable due to poaching and loss of habitat.

Elephants

In the Wild

The family of 14 elephants moved slowly along the river, eating leaves and branches of shrubs and trees. Mothers, daughters, calves, aunts, siblings, and grandmothers—they all followed the matriarch who had traveled the route hundreds of times before. She remembered the best place for foraging, the safest way to navigate the waterway, and how to avoid human settlements.

For two young calves, it was just another adventure. They butted heads, wrestled with their trunks, splashed each other in the river, and shook their ears at imaginary enemies. They chased each other up and down the slippery riverbank and slid into the water on their bellies. As they played, the calves never strayed far from the watchful eyes of their mothers.

At a secluded section of the river, the elephants stopped to feed on the dense vegetation along the river's edge. Some ended up in the river spraying water on their backs and bathing. Others rested and socialized. At the matriarch's signal, they all fell in behind her and disappeared into the forest. It was a noisy journey, full of roaring, trumpeting, and rumbling as they communicated with each other. By the next day, they were 30 kilometers (19 miles) away, foraging for food in a different part of their range.

In Captivity

In 1983, after her family was killed when elephant herds were culled in southern Africa, one-year-old Maggie was bought by the Alaska Zoo. She shared her quarters with Annabelle, the zoo's lone Asian elephant. In 1997, Annabelle died from a foot infection, and since that time, Maggie lived alone.

During the summer, Maggie's world was a small, outdoor pen of hard, compacted dirt and a shallow pond. During

Chris Lowthian/Born Free Foundation

Alaska's long winter, Maggie stood on an unheated concrete floor inside a 148-square meter (1600-square foot) barn. She was was overweight, sluggish, and had problems with dry skin. Several years after Annabelle's death, the zoo constructed a massive treadmill for Maggie to walk on. She never used it.

In May 2007, Maggie was found lying on her left side and couldn't get up. This is a dangerous position for an elephant. All that weight pushing down cuts off blood flow, impairs breathing, and damages organs and muscles. It took zookeepers, firefighters, and a towing company 19 hours to get Maggie on her feet again.

The zoo put Maggie on an hourly watch, but two days later she went down again for six hours. The zoo closed her exhibit and kept a keeper with her around the clock.

Meanwhile, a group of Anchorage citizens called Friends of Maggie stepped up their campaign to convince the zoo to move Maggie to a place with a warm climate, lots of space, and other elephants for companionship. The group met with zoo officials, organized Save Maggie rallies, and wrote to government officials. In November 2007, they were successful and Maggie was finally sent to a sanctuary in California. She is now doing very well.

Arthritis and Foot Rot

Arthritis and foot rot are common and serious ailments for zoo elephants. Both can end up as a deadly infection, and are caused by lack of exercise, overweight bodies, standing on hard soil and concrete floors, and cool, damp conditions. Wild elephants do not get arthritis or foot rot.

The Story of Keiko

The world's most famous orca is Keiko, who starred in the movie *Free Willy*. In 1979, when he wasn't yet two years old, Keiko was captured and taken to an aquarium in Iceland.

Mark Berman/www.keiko.com

Capturing Orcas

Since the 1960s, hundreds of orcas have been captured from the waters of Canada, the United States, Iceland, Japan, and Russia. It's a traumatic experience for the orcas. They're chased by high-speed boats, netted, wrestled into slings, hoisted up out of the water onto a boat, taken to shore, and dumped in shallow holding tanks.

Three years later, Keiko was shipped to Marineland in Niagara Falls, Ontario. He was bullied by the other whales, so in 1985, he was sold for $350,000 to an amusement park in Mexico City. In Mexico, Keiko lived in a small pool of warm water and performed tricks for visitors. He lost weight, his muscles deteriorated, and he developed a skin disease.

The world learned about Keiko's plight when *Free Willy* was released in 1993. Thousands of children wrote letters and campaigned to have Keiko set free. That helped convince Earth Island Institute, an environmental organization in San Francisco, to take on the enormous challenge of rehabilitating and releasing Keiko back into the wild.

In 1996, after more than a decade in Mexico, Keiko was flown to the Oregon Coast Aquarium and placed into a huge cold-water tank. For two years, he slowly gained weight, grew stronger, and learned how to catch fish. His skin disease disappeared.

In 1998, Keiko moved to a sea pen in Klettsvik Bay in Iceland, where he could experience the cold northern water, currents, wind, sun, and storms. He learned to leave his pen and follow a tracking boat out to sea. He met wild orcas and communicated with clicks and whistles.

Finally, Keiko swam free. He traveled 1600 km (1000 miles) to the Faroe Islands and then headed to Norway. He arrived heavier than he was when he left Iceland, a clear sign he'd been feeding well on the way.

In December 2003, Keiko died suddenly, probably from pneumonia. It was a sad day, but also a day when children and adults around the world celebrated Keiko's four years of freedom in the ocean.

Zoocheck Canada

Natural Facts

Home: Orcas inhabit all the oceans of the world. Their home ranges can cover tens of thousands of square kilometers of ocean.

Size: Male orcas can reach more than 9 meters (30 feet) in length, and weigh more than 6 tonnes (6.5 tons). Females are about 6.5 meters (21 feet), and weigh about 5 tonnes (5.5 tons).

Adaptations: Sleek and streamlined, orcas swim through more than 100 kilometers (60 miles) of ocean in just a few hours and descend into the depths. They have intelligence and sophisticated communication skills that help keep their families safe and together in great expanses of ocean.

Family Life: Female members of a family spend their lives together, and all share the job of raising calves. Closely related families form pods of 50-100 members from four or five generations. They hunt together and babysit for each other.

Conservation status: May be threatened due to pollution and depletion of fish stocks.

Great Apes

Gorillas, chimpanzees, and orangutans belong to the Great Ape family called Hominidae. Humans belong to the same family. All Hominidae use tools, form family and social groups, communicate, have long childhoods and lifespans, and share similar emotions.

In the Wild

Sitting on the rainforest floor, he heard the snap of stepped-on twigs and a deep, guttural voice. Suddenly, Dr. Kerry Bowman found himself face-to-face with a male silverback gorilla. He didn't look directly into the gorilla's eyes, fearing it might be perceived as a challenge. But he could feel the silverback's powerful presence and peacefulness. A few minutes later, the gorilla pushed his way back through the dense foliage and vanished.

Since the 1980s, Dr. Bowman has returned each year to the Democratic Republic of Congo to study eastern lowland gorillas in Kahuzi-Biega National Park, a stronghold for gorillas in the wild. The vast 600,000 hectares (1,480,000 acres) of forest and mountain are traditional gorilla habitat. Surveys in 1990 and 1996 showed that the park was home to about 285 gorillas divided into 25 family groups and a small number of solitary males. One of Dr. Bowman's study groups includes 28 family members of all ages.

Wild gorillas spend most of their day foraging. Family groups follow the silverback as they search for leaves, roots, fruit, shoots, and sometimes insects. Foraging isn't a stroll through the park. It involves digging, poking, and pulling; tearing and snapping vegetation apart; and maneu-

vering over, around, and through thickets and tree limbs. Two females in Dr. Bowman's study group carried twins as they foraged. Infants aren't carried on their mothers' backs until they are about four months old, so each mother carefully cradled two babies in her arms while moving through the forest.

With all their senses on high alert, the gorillas are constantly analyzing things and making decisions: how to handle obstacles; which tree has the best fruit; how to avoid venomous snakes; and how to socialize with other gorillas. They're also communicating as they move, passing on information and staying in touch.

In Captivity

The silverback leaned against a concrete tree and poked at his foot with a piece of straw. He tilted his head back, looked at me for a second, then went back to playing with the straw.

His exhibit was part of a Canadian zoo's $6-million African complex. The floors, walls, and trees were made of gunite, which is sprayed-on concrete. On the back wall was a mural of an African landscape with blue skies and fluffy clouds. Across the front were large windows. It looked a lot like a movie set.

In other zoos I've visited in warm climates, great apes were living in exhibits that were less costly but more naturalistic, with real trees, tall grasses, and large spaces. The apes there were more active and engaged. At the other extreme are the bare cages made of iron bars and stone where I've seen great apes living alone.

Natural Facts

Home: Gorillas and chimps live in the rainforest lowlands and mountains of equatorial Africa. Orangutans are native to the rainforests of Sumatra and Borneo.

Size: Gorilla males—180 kilograms (400 pounds); 1.7 meters (5.5 feet). Orangutan males—90 kilograms (198 pounds); 1 meter (3.2 feet). Male chimps—60 kilograms (130 pounds); 1.2 meters (4 feet) tall. Females are smaller.

Family Life: Apes live in families and social groups.

Conservation status: All great apes except humans are endangered due to habitat loss, illegal hunting, and logging.

Ian Redmond

Rob Laidlaw

CHAPTER 3

Around the Zoo World

A zoo is a place that keeps wild animals in captivity and exhibits them to the public. At last count, in 1993, the World Association of Zoos and Aquariums estimated that there were about 10,000 zoos around the world. If all kinds of zoos were counted, the number might be three times higher.

Safari park

Zoocheck Canada

Captive Places

The zoos most people know are big public zoos. But captive wild animals are exhibited in many other kinds of places.

Public Zoos

Big city zoos, like the Toronto Zoo and Bronx Zoo, are often owned by the public, funded by governments, and run by zoological societies. Some of them are involved in captive breeding, research, and education programs, and belong to associations that set their own standards for animal care.

24

Wildlife Sanctuaries and Conservation Centers

Sanctuaries offer lifetime care for captive wild animals who have been abused or retired. Conservation centers care for and breed endangered species. In both facilities, animal needs are the top priority. Sanctuaries and conservation centers are not in the business of exhibiting animals, but some are open to visitors.

The Association of Sanctuaries in the U.S. sets high standards of animal welfare. Each elephant, for example, must be provided with 87,000 square feet (8000 square meters) of outdoor space and at least five companions. Sanctuary animals cannot be bred, bought, sold, or traded.

Wild Animal Parks

Wild animal parks are zoos where animals live in large, open enclosures. Whipsnade Park in England covers 243 hectares (600 acres). The San Diego Wild Animal Park in the U.S. sits on 728 hectares (1800 acres).

Aquariums and Marine Parks

Aquariums are zoos that keep aquatic animals in pools and tanks. Many feature performing whales, dolphins, and sea lions. Some belong to associations with their own standards for animal care.

Roadside Zoos

Roadside zoos are located on rural roads and on highways outside cities. They are privately owned businesses that keep small collections of animals, usually confined in homemade cages and enclosures.

Safari Park Zoos

Safari parks are drive-through zoos, usually with an African theme. "Caged" in their cars, visitors travel through enclosures of "free-roaming" animals. Safari parks are often privately owned and fund their operations with ticket sales.

Other Zoos

Other kinds of zoos include aviaries and bird parks, reptile zoos, butterfly gardens, and insectariums.

Zoo Evolution

The first zoo I visited confined animals in small cages behind heavy bars or in barren grottoes surrounded by high walls. The Riverdale Zoo dated back to 1894, and those concrete cages and grottoes were a legacy of the early days of zookeeping when public zoos kept their animals in barred concrete cages.

Back then, few people recognized how much harm the zoos were inflicting on the animals. There weren't field scientists, like Jane Goodall or Winnie Kiiru, studying animals in the wild. How animals lived in their natural habitats was still a mystery.

Public zoos of the nineteenth and early twentieth centuries were designed for visitors and zookeepers, not for wild animals. A cage made of concrete made cleaning easier for zookeepers. Exhibiting animals behind bars or in open grottoes ensured that zoo visitors could see the animals all the time, and that's why people came to the zoo.

In many modern zoos, living conditions for wild animals haven't changed since the late nineteenth century when animals were confined behind bars in small concrete cages.

Zoos Without Bars

In 1908, an animal dealer named Carl Hagenbeck opened his own zoo, called Tierpark Hagenbeck, near Hamburg, Germany. The years Hagenbeck spent in wild places around the world collecting animals gave him new ideas about how they should be displayed. Tierpark Hagenbeck was the first zoo that confined animals with moats and ditches, instead of behind bars and fences. It was also the first zoo that shaped concrete into rocks and mountains and painted landscapes on walls to create the illusion of a natural habitat.

Hagenback's ideas were slow to catch on, but eventually more zoos moved their animals into open-style exhibits surrounded by moats. The new exhibits were larger but still barren and undersized. And entertaining zoo visitors by providing wide open views was still more important than meeting the needs of the animals.

Rob Laidlaw

The features in this modern Hagenbeck-style orangutan exhibit are made of hard molded concrete called gunite.

Zoo Revolution

One of the most famous people in America in the 1920s and 1930s was Frank Buck. A swashbuckling adventurer who sported a pencil mustache and a pith helmet, Buck traveled to the jungles of South America, Africa, and Asia capturing elephants, tigers, lions, leopards, monkeys, reptiles, and birds. He loaded them on ships and sold them to zoos and circuses. Animal dealers, like Frank Buck and Carl Hagenbeck, took as many animals as they wanted from anywhere in the world.

By the 1960s, so many wild animals had been captured for the fur and pet trade that some species were facing extinction. That led to an international agreement to control trade in wild animals and plant species. In 1973, at a meeting organized by the World Conservation Union, 21 countries signed the Convention on International Trade in Endangered Species of Wild Fauna

The white rhino was on CITES list of endangered animals in 1974. They're still on CITES Red List of Threatened Species, which now includes 5000 animal species. By 2007, more than 170 countries had signed CITES.

Rob Laidlaw

and Flora (CITES). They agreed to control the exporting and importing of animals that appeared on the CITES list of species that needed protection.

CITES helped cause a change in the zoo world in the 1970s. Because it was harder to buy certain animals captured in the wild, zoos started breeding them in captivity. Today some zoos claim to be saving endangered species through captive breeding.

Breeding in Captivity

Some zoos are involved in co-operative efforts to breed endangered animals in captivity. Members of the U.S. Association of Zoos and Aquariums are involved in more than 100 Species Survival Plans. European zoos have Endangered Species Breeding Programs, and zoos in Australia have Species Management Plans.

Captive breeding is not an effective or useful conservation tool for most species and most of these programs just breed animals for zoo displays. Only a small number of species, such as the Arabian oryx and California condor, have ever been released to the wild.

Captive breeding has another big downside—too many babies and surplus animals. Most zoo breeding produces animals who are already common in captivity, so it's hard to find them permanent homes, especially males who may be aggressive when they get older. Some zoos sell, trade, or loan their surplus animals to other zoos. When that's not possible, they may sell their surplus animals to animal dealers or into the pet trade.

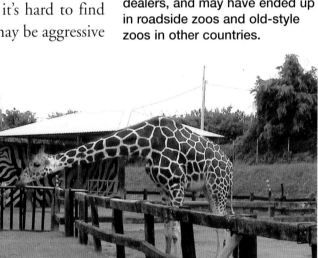

In 1995, more than 40 American zoos had giraffes for sale, and no other public zoos wanted them. Some went to animal dealers, and may have ended up in roadside zoos and old-style zoos in other countries.

Rob Laidlaw

Public Zoos

Many public zoos are big, complicated places, with thousands of animals, dozens of zookeepers, a team of veterinarians, restaurants, shops, and zoo trains. They may be involved in breeding animals, and a few help with conservation projects in the field. Major-league zoos host huge crowds of students every year and open their gates to millions of visitors.

Zoo Standards

Many zoos belong to associations, such as the U.S. Association of Zoos and Aquariums (AZA). To become a member, a zoo must pass an inspection based on the association's standards. Some of those standards focus on animal care.

It's good to have zoo standards, but some of them don't seem very good for the animals. To get AZA's seal of approval, 167.2 square meters (1800 square feet) of outdoor space—the size of a parking lot that holds nine cars—is all that's required for one elephant, and half that amount for each companion. AZA recommends at least two companions for each female elephant, but this is a recommendation rather than a rule.

This gorilla exhibit is filled with gunite rocks, cliffs, and trees. The real trees are wrapped in electrified wires.

Zoocheck Canada

Immersion Exhibits

Many zoos are constructing new exhibits that look like natural ecosystems—from the Serengeti savanna to a Brazilian rainforest. Called immersion exhibits, they're supposed to make visitors feel they're in the wild with the animals.

In old-zoo days, lions lived beside other big cats and penguins with other penguins. In immersion exhibits, species who share the same habitats may be displayed side by side. Recorded sounds of chirping birds or chittering monkeys are piped in, and trees, plants, and rocks disguise barriers and equipment.

These multi-million dollar, high-tech exhibits sometimes look a bit more natural, but many animals are no better off. Rocks are usually made of gunite, and real trees and plants are encased in electrified wires. Animals get a shock when they touch them and learn very quickly to stay away.

Zoos that belong to the U.S. Association of Zoos and Aquariums can keep one elephant in an outdoor space that's the size of a parking lot for nine cars. The AZA standard is thousands of times smaller than the space wild elephants use.

Jo-Anne McArthur/Zoocheck Canada

Goodnight, Yupi

On a hot day in 2005, I arrived at one of Mexico's public zoos to visit a polar bear named Yupi. I spotted a high white wall, sculpted to resemble ice and snow. No doubt this was the home of Yupi, a female polar bear orphaned in Alaska in 1993. She was lying flat in the middle of a concrete floor, trying to stay cool.

Two days later, I was allowed to see Yupi in her night quarters. The zookeeper showed me a tiny, concrete room. This is where Yupi lived when the zoo was closed, from 5 o'clock in the evening to 9 or 10 o'clock the next morning. It was hot and humid inside. There was nothing to play with, no bedding to lie on, and only two small, barred windows.

I peered through the bars. Yupi looked back at me, and I could feel her breath on my face. I felt sorry for this magnificent animal, and angry at all the zoos that put animals into small, barren cages when visitors go home.

When the zoo is closed, Yupi lives in a small concrete room behind a barred steel door.

Roadside Zoos

I had a sinking feeling when I pulled off the road in rural Ontario. The owner of a horse farm had set up a roadside zoo on his property, and things didn't look good as I surveyed the homemade, rickety cages.

Near the back of the property was a lopsided shed with a screen door hanging loose. Inside was a Hamadryas baboon. She was huddled at the back of a wire cage barely larger than a closet. The baboon was holding a dirty piece of apple, and when I spoke to her, she dropped it and shuffled towards me. She reached her hand through the wire and grasped my fingers. I looked at her closely and realized she was blind.

I reported the baboon's terrible living conditions to the humane society. When I returned to the zoo, she was gone, and I never found out what happened to her. That lonely baboon was just one wild animal out of thousands who each year show up in, or disappear from, roadside zoos in North America.

A dog and a lion share a small, dirty cage during the winter at a roadside zoo in Canada.

Horrible Lives

Animals in roadside zoos live in horrible conditions: small, dilapidated cages and enclosures; pens with no shelter from the weather; floors filthy with droppings; nocturnal animals kept in bright light; social animals living alone; inadequate food and water.

Most owners of roadside zoos don't know how to care for their animals. Few have any training or enough money. Government inspections are rare, and there aren't many laws protecting the welfare of wild animals in private zoos.

At one place, I saw a jaguar living in an old, narrow, walk-in bird cage. The barren space was so small he could only turn around by scrunching up his body and lifting his front paws off the floor. His constant pacing had compacted the ground into a hard, concrete-like surface called hardpan. These are conditions I see far too often.

In the wild, Japanese macaques live in large troops in forested areas. This one lives in a roadside zoo in Ontario. In Ontario, anyone can buy tigers and macaques from an animal dealer or wildlife auction, stick them in homemade cages, and open a zoo.

Zoocheck Canada

Dangerous Places

Every year, animals in zoos escape from their cages and endanger the lives of visitors, neighbors, and themselves. In May 2007, a woman was mauled to death by a tiger who reached out of his cage at a small display in British Columbia. In December 2007, one man was killed and two others injured when a tiger escaped from her cage at the San Francisco Zoo. There is even a zoo that allows people to kiss a grizzly bear. Separated by an electric wire, visitors let the bear reach out and lick their face. One bite or paw swipe and someone could be killed. It's one of the most potentially dangerous things I've seen in a zoo.

Too Many Babies

A few years ago, I visited one of the largest wild animal auctions in the U.S. Along the side of the road were hundreds of trucks emblazoned with the names of private zoos and animal dealers. Almost 10,000 animals were packed into the sprawling complex of barns and tents, including miniature ponies, zebras, black bears, and a white tiger. They sold for bargain-basement prices to dealers, owners of roadside zoos, and people who wanted an exotic pet. That's what happens when too many babies are born in zoos, including the big zoos, every year—and when there are few laws to protect them.

Rob Laidlaw

This lion cub faces a terrible fate living in a roadside zoo or as a pet in someone's backyard. In Ontario and many other places, anyone can buy a lion for a pet— no licence required and no questions asked. Tigers are a popular exotic pet because they breed well in captivity. Some people estimate that 15,000 pet tigers live in backyards and basements in North America.

CHAPTER 4

An Elephant Step in the Right Direction

The Story of Wanda and Winky

On a visit to the Detroit Zoo in 2003, I stopped to see Wanda and Winky. The female Asian elephants were standing in a dusty yard much smaller than a football field. They shuffled around, a few steps in one direction, then a few steps in another. They rocked back and forth and scraped the hard ground with their feet. Wanda and Winky didn't look happy, and they didn't act like elephants I've watched in the wild.

Wanda was 44 years old and Winky was 50. Wanda had arthritis in her front legs, so her joints ached whenever she moved. Every day, she took medicine for her pain and swollen joints. Winky had a foot infection, which was being treated with antibiotics and painkillers. She didn't lie down to sleep at night because it hurt too much to lower her body and then stand up again.

In 2004, Ron Kagan, the director of the Detroit Zoo, decided that Wanda and Winky were suffering too much. He announced that the zoo would retire them to an elephant sanctuary—a peaceful place with warm winters, wide-open spaces, and more companions. "Improving things for the elephants," Ron Kagan said, "really meant not having them."

The zoo that owned Wanda wanted her and Winky moved to another zoo, and so did the Association of Zoos and Aquariums. That's when hundreds of people across the country started speaking out to save the elephants from living the rest of their days cooped up in a zoo. In the end, the elephants won.

In April 2005, Wanda and Winky arrived at the ARK2000 captive wildlife sanctuary in San Andreas, California. Today, they live with five other Asian elephants on 14 hectares (35 acres) of rolling hills and woodlands, digging in the dirt and dozing in the sun—acting like real elephants. Winky now sleeps lying down every night.

"The zoo is the window into our humanity and how we treat other things in nature."

—Ron Kagan,
director of the Detroit Zoo

The story doesn't end here. In 2005, after 81 years of keeping elephants, the Detroit Zoo closed its elephant exhibit forever—because life in a city zoo isn't a good life for elephants. Since then, other elephants have been moved out of zoos and into wildlife sanctuaries.

I hope this is a sign that the zoo world is starting to change by putting the welfare of the animals first. All wild animals in captivity deserve active and healthy lives filled with the freedom to act naturally. Putting the needs of the animal first—that's the most important thing zoos of the future can do.

Wanda and Winky enjoying their retirement at the ARK2000 Captive Wildlife Sanctuary in San Andreas, California

The Future of Zoos

Ron Kagan's decision to close Detroit's elephant exhibit forever was a big step in the right direction—where caring for the welfare of individual animals is the most important thing zoos can do. But we have a long way to go to change the way most zoos operate and to stop the suffering of wild animals in captivity.

Luckily, we have a new breed of specialist facilities and a handful of progressive zoos that are good models for the future. They show that it's possible to provide rescued, retired, and a small number of endangered, animals a pleasant life in a natural setting; that conservation goals can be achieved with ingenuity and modest budgets; and that wildlife facilities can play a role in conservation education.

Arizona-Sonora Desert Museum

You won't find a panda or a polar bear pacing back and forth in the Arizona-Sonora Desert Museum—no exotic animals

allowed. Often called the world's best zoo, it exhibits 300 animal and 1200 plant species that are all native to the Sonora Desert, which extends from Arizona and California into Mexico. Mountain lions, bobcats, prairie dogs, coyotes, jaguars, big-horned sheep, badgers, bats, javelinas, otters, and owls live in interesting, naturalistic habitats. Most famous inhabitants: the saguaro cactus and the Gila monster. The museum also has an impressive education program, with interactive displays and volunteers who inspire visitors to appreciate the magic of the Sonora Desert.

Jersey Zoo

Gerald Durrell was a man ahead of his time. When his Jersey Zoo opened in 1959, it wasn't just another zoo. Durrell focused on breeding small endangered species and returning them to the wild—on conservation rather than entertainment. In the early 1970s, pink pigeons and Mauritius kestrels teetered on the brink of extinction. Durrell's captive breeding and conservation work helped the wild populations grow and remove the kestrel from the endangered list. Located on an island in the English Channel, the renamed Durrell Wildlife Conservation Trust exhibits 190 species of native and exotic animals—from jumping rats and meerkats to aye-ayes and pygmy hogs—in stimulating, complex enclosures.

Mountain View Conservation and Breeding Centre

At the Mountain View Conservation and Breeding Centre near Fort Langley, British Columbia, 24 African painted dogs race through their paddocks and then settle down to rest and socialize.

When founder Gordon Blankstein discovered painted dogs were endangered, he started breeding them for release. He has had success in the past. Small herds of Addax and Cuvier's gazelles bred at the center now roam wild in Africa. At Mountain View, small numbers of visitors get a chance to see 50 of the world's rarest species—from kulans and Mountain bongos to Indian desert cats and Vancouver Island marmots.

The China Bear Rescue Center

Seven thousand bears are confined in tiny, steel cages on farms in China. They have been captured to supply bile (an internal fluid) for the Traditional Chinese Medicine Industry. More than 200 of the "bile bears" have been rescued by the Animals Asia Foundation and placed into the China Bear Rescue Center, one of the world's most remarkable sanctuaries. Many come with severe injuries and health problems. They are given veterinary care and time to heal. Then they are released into large compounds, where they can run, climb, swim, or play with other bears. The sanctuary welcomes organized visitor groups twice a month and has plans for an education village to help visitors understand bears and why they should be protected.

Animals Asia Foundation

The Elephant Sanctuary

The world-famous Elephant Sanctuary sits on 1100 hectares (2700 acres) near Hohenwald, Tennessee, and provides a permanent refuge to elephants who have been retired from zoos and circuses. Founded in 1995 by Carol Buckley, who had trained elephants for the circus, and former zookeeper Scott Blais, the sanctuary has a unique philosophy. It is rooted in the belief that the care and management of captive elephants should be dictated by the nature of the elephants themselves and not by human needs or available resources. The sanctuary cares for more than 20 elephants who can only be viewed through video cameras.

Winky (left) with her friends Shirley, Jenny, and Bunny

Fred Clarke. Used with permission The Elephant Sanctuary in Tennessee

Checking Up on Zoos

Captive wild animals should live in as large a space as possible, with lots of room to explore and act naturally, soft soil under their feet, and private places to escape from people and other animals. But they need much more. If any of their physical or behavioral needs are not met, they may be suffering and need our help.

I've walked through hundreds of zoos around the world checking up on the welfare of their animals. No matter where I am or what animals I'm looking at, I start with a series of questions—questions you can ask wherever you see wild animals living in captivity. The first and most important is, "Should these animals be here at all?" Most times, the answer is no.

Three Critical Questions

Q Are animals living in cramped quarters that prevent normal, natural movement?

Q Do they spend most of their time on hard surfaces or wire floors?

Q Are they living in a barren cage with no structures to climb, furnishings to use, or objects to explore?

These are the first things I look at in every zoo I visit because they reveal critical problems. If the answer is yes to just one of these questions, an animal's whole well-being is at risk.

Q Do the animals look injured, sick, or in poor condition with missing fur, feathers, or scales?

Q Are their hooves, claws, or teeth overgrown?

Q Are they sitting in one spot, lying down, or sleeping all the time?

Q Are they pacing or rocking back and forth, constantly licking things, or displaying other abnormal behaviors?

If you see these signs, it means an animal may be suffering physically and mentally and needs veterinary care, more space, and something to do.

Q Are animals from a tropical rainforest receiving the same sunlight, humidity, and temperature they get in the wild?

Q Are arctic animals living in a hot climate with no relief from heat and high humidity?

Q Are desert animals exposed to heavy rain and frigid temperatures?

Over thousands of years, species have adapted to specific environments, so they require the same conditions in captivity.

This gharial lives on hard-packed earth in a barren cage with nowhere to go and nothing to do.

Rob Laidlaw

10 Ways to Help Wild Animals in Captivity

1. Report captive wild animals living in poor or cruel conditions to the humane society, wildlife protection groups, government agencies, and local politicians. Your report should include a written description and photos.

Rob Laidlaw

2. Investigate how wild animals are used by some zoos and aquariums to perform tricks—from elephants walking tightropes to sea lions tooting horns. Some zoos have stopped making animals do stunts for visitors.

3. Create a display at your school that shows how some zoo animals suffer and why it is important to challenge the way that many zoos house and care for their animals.

4. Start a letter-writing campaign to voice your concerns about roadside zoos and other facilities that neglect or exploit captive animals. Send letters to newspapers, governments, animal welfare groups, and zoo owners.

5. Support wildlife sanctuaries that provide permanent homes to retired or neglected animals. Research the facility first because some places just call themselves sanctuaries. Real sanctuaries care for animals for the rest of their lives.

6. Join a wildlife group that helps save animals in their natural habitats.

7. Inform your friends about the special needs of elephants, polar bears, dolphins and whales, and Great Apes—and why these wide-ranging animals do poorly in captivity.

8. Many zoos ask the public for money to help build new cages (often called habitats). If you want to help captive animals, donate money to a sanctuary instead.

9. If you want to see wildlife, visit sanctuaries or specialist facilities, or best of all, start visiting parks and natural areas. Bring binoculars and a guide book. You'll learn a lot and become healthier as well.

10. Get involved in an organization that is devoted to protecting wild animals in captivity. The list of animal welfare groups on page 46 is a good place to start.

Animal Welfare Organizations

For more information about wild animals in captivity, you may want to contact these organizations.

Animal Concerns Research and Education Society
www.acres.org.sg

Animals Asia Foundation
www.animalsasia.org

Born Free Foundation
www.bornfree.org.uk

Compassionate Crusaders Trust
animalcrusaders.org/door.html

Elephant Sanctuary
www.elephants.com

Environment and Animal Society of Taiwan
www.east.org.tw

Humane Society of the United States
www.hsus.org

In Defense of Animals
www.idausa.org

International Primate Protection League
www.ippl.org

People for the Ethical Treatment of Animals
www.peta.org
www.petaindia.com

Performing Animal Welfare Society
www.pawsweb.org

ProFauna Indonesia
www.profauna.or.id

SOS fauna
www.sosfauna.org

Tacugama Chimpanzee Sanctuary
www.tacugama.com

World Society for the Protection of Animals (WSPA)
www.wspa.org.uk

Zoocheck Canada
www.zoocheck.com

Glossary

Adaptations: physical and behavioral traits that help animals and plants survive in a habitat

Animal welfare: health and well-being of animals

Arthritis: joint disease

Association of Zoos and Aquariums: organization that accredits zoos and aquariums

Captivity: wild animals confined in zoos, in private parks, in circuses, and by exotic pet owners

Conservation status: risk of extinction of animals and plants

Convention on International Trade in Endangered Species of Wild Fauna and Flora (CITES): agreement to protect certain species of animals and plants from exploitation through international trade

Endangered species: population of animals and plants threatened by environmental changes

Environmental enrichment: attempt to provide zoo animals with opportunities for exercise and natural behavior

Foot rot: infection that affects animal's hoof

Five Freedoms of Animal Welfare: the freedoms all animals need for a good life

Gunite: molded concrete used in animal exhibits

Immersion exhibit: attempt to create for zoo visitors the sights and sounds of a natural-looking environment

Natural habitat: home where animal or plant lives in the wild

Stereotypies: abnormal, repetitive behaviors

Wildlife sanctuary: refuge for neglected, abused, unwanted, or retired animals

World Association of Zoos and Aquariums: umbrella organization of the international community of zoos and aquariums

Index

47

Text copyright © 2008 by Rob Laidlaw

Published in Canada by
Fitzhenry & Whiteside,
195 Allstate Parkway,
Markham, Ontario L3R 4T8

Published in the United States by
Fitzhenry & Whiteside,
311 Washington Street,
Brighton, Massachusetts 02135

www.fitzhenry.ca   godwit@fitzhenry.ca

Library and Archives Canada Cataloguing in Publication
Laidlaw, Rob
    Wild animals in captivity / Rob Laidlaw.
ISBN 978-1-55455-025-8
1. Captive wild animals—Juvenile literature.   2. Animal welfare—
Juvenile literature.   I. Title.
QL77.5.L33 2007   j636.088'9   C2007-902283-9

U.S. Publisher Cataloging-in-Publication Data
(Library of Congress Standards)
Laidlaw, Rob.
    Wild animals in captivity / Rob Laidlaw.
[48] p. : col. ill. ; cm.
Summary: An eye-opening look at how zoo-life affects the health and behavior of wild animals, including elephants, polar bears, whales, and apes.
ISBN-13: 978-1-55455-025-8
1. Captive wild animals — Juvenile literature. 2. Zoos — Juvenile literature.
3. Zoo animals — Juvenile literature.
I. Title.
590.744 dc22   QL77.5.L353 2007

Fitzhenry & Whiteside acknowledges with thanks the Canada Council for the Arts, and the Ontario Arts Council for their support of our publishing program. We acknowledge the financial support of the Government of Canada through the Book Publishing Industry Development Program (BPIDP) for our publishing activities.

Canada Council   Conseil des Arts
for the Arts   du Canada

ONTARIO ARTS COUNCIL
CONSEIL DES ARTS DE L'ONTARIO

Design by Fortunato Design Inc.

Cover photo credits: front cover, Rob Laidlaw; author photo, Zoocheck Canada

Printed in China

10 9 8 7 6 5 4 3 2 1